A Word About This Book

This book doesn't really need a long introduction from me because its whole purpose is to let God speak directly to you from his Word. It is basically a collection of the wonderful promises God has made to us and the wonderful ways he blesses us—along with a little commentary about how these promises and blessings have touched my life.

It might help you to know, if you don't know already, that as I prepared this book I was undergoing treatment for cancer. I often felt weak or low or in pain from the treatments or the side effects of the disease. But I'm not telling you this so you'll feel sorry for me. I know you have your own set of problems, your own pain that you must endure. And these promises and blessings are for you, too. I pray they will uplift you and give you hope, just as they have done for me.

You see, in the midst of this very difficult time of my life, I have been reminded and assured again and again of some very basic and very comforting truths:

First, our God keeps his promises. We can absolutely depend on it. If he's said it, he's going to do it, and often he'll do it in a way that leaves us openmouthed with awe.

Second, God is continually in the process of showering us with blessings. He loves to give good gifts to his children. He loves *us*. So that's another thing we can absolutely depend on. If we trust God, he will fill our lives with goodness—often in surprising ways.

And third, God remains dependable and good no matter what is happening to us at the moment—whether we are aware of what God is doing or not. Sometimes it seems as if he's not even there! But we will find out eventually what he's been up to—either down the road a bit, or when we need it most, or when we go to live in eternity with him. And then we'll realize anew that no matter what has happened to us, we've always been safe in the Father's hands.

Because that's true, I really believe the most appropriate word for us to speak every day of our lives, regardless of what seems to be going on—is "Thank you." We need to say it again and again. When those words are on our lips, we'll keep our hearts in the praise position—open—and then we'll be much more aware of the many ways God is working out his promises in our lives and showering us with beautiful blessings.

Love,
Emilie Barnes

GOOD AND *Perfect*

On several occasions, my doctor has used the term "divine intervention" after we have changed something about my treatment. Perhaps my tests weren't positive, and he had to do something different because of some changes in my blood chemistry—or he had to try something new because something else had gone wrong with my course of treatment. Each time this has happened, plan two turned out to be more productive than what either of us originally anticipated. "Divine intervention" was the doctor's way of expressing to me that God has a higher plan and God's plans are better than what the doctor was going to do. And of course I know that's true—both of my medical treatment and of my life in general!

I just look upward and say, "Thank you, God, for all your good and perfect gifts."

Every good gift and every perfect gift is from above, and comes down from the Father of lights, with whom there is no variation or shadow of turning.

JAMES 1:17 NKJV

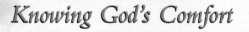

Knowing God's Comfort

Safe in the Father's Hands

EMILIE BARNES

artwork by CAROLYN SHORES WRIGHT

HARVEST HOUSE PUBLISHERS
Eugene, Oregon

Safe in the Father's Hands

Text Copyright © 2001 by Emilie Barnes
Published by Harvest House Publishers
Eugene, Oregon 97402

Barnes, Emilie.
   Safe in the Father's hands / Emilie Barnes ; artwork by Carolyn Shores Wright.
      p. cm.
   ISBN 0-7369-0435-2
   1. Cancer–Patients–Religious life. 2. Barnes, Emilie. 3. Cancer–Religious aspects–Christianity. 4. Consolation. I. Title.

BV4910.33 .B37 2001
242`.4–dc21   00-059749

Artwork designs are reproduced under license from © Arts Uniq' ®, Inc., Cookeville, TN and may not be reproduced without permission. For more information regarding art prints featured in this book, please contact:

> Arts Uniq'
> P.O. Box 3085
> Cookeville, TN 38502
> 1.800.223.5020

Design and production by Garborg Design Works, Minneapolis, Minnesota

For more information regarding speaking engagements and additional material from Emilie Barnes, please send a self-addressed envelope to:

> **More Hours in My Day**
> 2838 Rumsey Drive
> Riverside, CA 92506

Or you can visit us on the Internet at: www.emiliebarnes.com or emilie@emiliebarnes.com.

Harvest House Publishers has made every effort to trace the ownership of all poems and quotes. In the event of a question arising from the use of a poem or quote, we regret any error made and will be pleased to make the necessary correction in future editions of this book.

Scripture quotations marked NIV are taken from the Holy Bible, New International Version®, Copyright © 1973, 1978, 1984 by the International Bible Society. Used by permission of Zondervan Publishing House; Scripture quotations marked NASB are from the New American Standard Bible®, ©1960, 1962, 1971, 1972, 1973, 1975, 1977 by The Lockman Foundation. Used by permission. Scripture quotations marked NKJV are from the New King James Version, Copyright © 1982 by Thomas Nelson, Inc. Used by permission. All rights reserved. Scripture quotations marked TLB are from The Living Bible Copyright © 1971. Used by permission of Tyndale House Publishers, Inc., Wheaton, Illinois 60189. All rights reserved. Scripture quotations marked NRSV are from the New Revised Standard Version of the Bible, Copyright © 1989 by the Division of Christian Education of the National Council of the Churches of Christ in the USA. Used by permission.

Printed in Hong Kong.

01 02 03 04 05 06 07 08 09 10 / NG / 10 9 8 7 6 5 4 3 2 1

I CAN *Depend* ON GOD

As I wake each new morning, I can be assured that my heavenly Father will be the same that day as the one before. Even though others might fail me, he will never let me down. I am confident when I approach his throne that I will be in his presence. I am never left out. When I pray to him, he listens.

God has a past record of hearing all of my prayers and answering. He hasn't always responded to them as quickly as I might have liked, and his answers were not always the ones I wanted to hear. But he has never failed to give me what I needed—and more.

The LORD… is righteous; he does no wrong. Morning by morning he dispenses his justice, and every new day he does not fail.

ZEPHANIAH 3:5 NIV

I need to remember that on those mornings (and evenings) when God seems far away. No matter how it feels, he's listening. I can always count on God.

God's Timetable

One of the great accomplishments of life is learning to find rest in our appointed time—relishing the joys and challenges that come with each new stage of living—the excitement and possibilities of youth, the satisfaction and fulfillment of maturity, the wisdom and patience of later years. As we advance in age, though we see our youth and its aspirations flee by, we are given wonderful memories to cherish and new lessons to learn, and we anticipate more and more eagerly the time of being with the Lord for eternity.

There is an appointed time for everything. And there is a time for every event under heaven.... He has made everything appropriate in its time.

ECCLESIASTES 3:1, 11 NASB

I have learned that God has a master plan for my life—and there's great comfort in knowing it's his timetable I live by. I have already experienced so many of his seasons—and each one has been good in its own way. Why shouldn't I expect the next stage to be good as well?

A Harvest of *Love*

It's a well-known (and biblical) principle: Whatever we sow, we reap. The harvest always comes after the planting. All other things being equal, we can anticipate that with good weather and adequate rain, we will have a large crop—that is, if we have made the effort to sow in the first place.

In a sense, I am experiencing that harvesttime in my life right now. I am reaping the results of friendship seeds sown in other seasons. I remember busy times when I almost didn't have time for friends—when a phone call or a note or a luncheon date or even a word of prayer was truly a sacrifice of my time, when making time for others was truly a struggle.

But how glad I am that I made those efforts

Yes, I am the Vine; you are the branches. Whoever lives in me and I in him shall produce a large crop of fruit. For apart from me you can't do a thing.

JOHN 15:5 TLB

to sow seeds of friendship and love and to cultivate those love crops carefully—for now I have the privilege of reaping an abundant harvest. I'm so blessed to have all my family, friends, and loved ones around me during this time of my life. Through my friends' expressions of love and kindness, Christ has been shared with me.

God HAS A PLAN

The psalmist expressed it so beautifully: "For You formed my inward parts; You covered me in my mother's womb. I will praise You, for I am fearfully and wonderfully made..." (Psalm 139:13-14 NKJV).

What a blessing to remember what those words mean! Without God I would not even have existed. God planned for me a long time ago, and he has had a plan for my life even before I was born—before my mother had even thought to name me Emilie Marie. I just pray that I have done what I could to fulfill those plans, so that I can stand before him some day and hear him say, "Well done, good and faithful servant" (Matthew 25:23 NKJV).

O, LORD, you are my God;
I will exalt you and praise your name,
for in perfect faithfulness
you have done marvelous things,
things planned long ago.

ISAIAH 25:1 NIV

A REAL *Princess*

Galatians 4 contains one of my favorite promises in Scripture. I marvel to think that I am a child of God with all the full rights of being his heir. Just think— even though I wasn't born into one of the world's richest families, I still get to share in the richest inheritance of all—being part of God's eternal kingdom!

During my many hours of being alone in a hospital bed, I have had plenty of quiet time to think about this abundance of riches that I have inherited. I stand in awe—even when I'm lying down— to think of what Jesus did for me on the cross and what his sacrifice meant in terms of my inheritance. He made a real princess out of me—for I'm the rightful daughter of the King of kings.

But when the time had fully come, God sent his Son, born of a woman, born under law, to redeem those under law, that we might receive the full rights of sons.

GALATIANS 4:4,5 NIV

WHERE *Joy* COMES FROM

rue joy does not come from material possessions, even though they can be wonderful and enjoyable. It does not come from having a healthy family or a successful career, although those can be meaningful and fulfilling. It doesn't come from physical pleasure or delighting the senses. All those things can be good, but eventually they will be gone. Real joy—the kind that lasts forever—comes from steadfast trust in the Lord. Through good times and bad times, through sickness and health, through all sorts of ups and downs, we can still express honest joy—because we belong to God, because he has saved us from our sins, because he has ultimate control over what happens to us, and because we know we can trust him to make all things good.

Though the fig tree does not bud
and there are no grapes on the vines,
though the olive crop fails
and the fields produce no food…
yet I will rejoice in the LORD,
I will be joyful in God my savior.

HABAKKUK 3:17,18 NIV

GOOD NEWS FOR *Eternity*

*H*ow can I help but rejoice when I'm reminded that I serve a living God and that he will endure forever?

As I read the national and local news and I hear of all the persecutions of believers around the world, I claim this promise that his kingdom will not be destroyed. Not ever. Not by anything that human beings or the powers of darkness can do—and some of those things are pretty bad!

As I look back over the last six thousand years of history I find confidence that God has always been in the business of rescuing men and women from the clutches of evil and from our own selfishness and sin.

> *For he is the living God*
> *and he endures forever;*
> *his kingdom will not be destroyed,*
> *his dominion will never end.*
> *He rescues and he saves;*
> *he performs signs and wonders*
> *in the heavens and on the earth.*
>
> DANIEL 6:26,27 NIV

God is eternal and everlasting. He always has been, and he will always be. What a blessed assurance!

Full *Confidence*

The term *hope* is a much stronger word in the original than our present day "hope." The initial meaning stresses the confidence that one has in the Lord. Not like today's casual meaning of "I wish" or anticipate it to be true. No, we can have the fullest confidence that God is our helper and our shield. I know that nothing comes into my life until God has had an opportunity to review it first. In all things I look to God and ask, "What are you trying to teach me through this situation?" I know that every event of our life appears for a purpose of good. I'm trying real hard to understand that particular mystery of life.

We wait in hope for the LORD; he is our help and our shield.

PSALM 33:20 NIV

Love *Beyond* COMPREHENSION

There must be a lot of people who love me! I've come to believe that because so many people have said that they would take my disease from me if they could—even take my illness upon themselves to spare me. Some of these expressions have come from people I would never have expected. And they really mean it! Tears come to my eyes when I think of how much they would willingly sacrifice for my sake.

But that kind of sacrifice—multiplied many times—is exactly what Jesus made for us all when he took our place on the cross. Our sins were nailed to that cross when he was crucified. How he must have loved us to endure that terrible death for our sake.

> *This is My commandment, that you love one another, just as I have loved you. Greater love has no one than this, that one lay down his life for his friends.*
>
> JOHN 15:12,13 NASB

The depth of that love is beyond my comprehension. There's nothing I can do to deserve it or repay it. All I can do is say "thank you"—and try to pass it on.

A THOUSAND TIMES *Blessed*

To know that my blessings will be increased a thousand times is almost beyond my comprehension. After all, though a bank might give me 5.5 percent interest on my savings, a thousand percent markup is simply unbelievable. Yet that is exactly what I am promised in Deuteronomy 1:11. The Lord has promised to increase my blessings—and your blessings—a thousandfold!

Of course, this verse is talking about more than money. It's also talking about a return on my investment in family, emotional stability, marriage, health, desires, and all other components of life. And it doesn't have a time limit, either. Perhaps some of the blessings I'm promised will happen in eternity and in the lives of those who come after me on this earth.

Still, I know that God keeps his promises—and what a promise this is! It really helps to realize my blessings are growing and growing and growing—even amid the uncertainties of my present situation.

May the LORD, the God of your fathers, increase you a thousand times and bless you as he has promised!

DEUTERONOMY 1:11 NIV

Ever-Faithful

I came to know the Lord at age sixteen, and I have never really turned away from him. All of my writings have this theme of faithfulness woven through them, and many readers have told me they are blessed by it.

But faithfulness isn't always easy! Each day I have to recommit to that youthful decision. Each day I struggle to maintain the discipline of Scripture reading and prayer, of taking myself off the throne and trusting God with my life. During this time of physical testing the struggle is sometimes even harder because of sheer physical weakness and pain.

Sometimes, despite my best efforts, I've let the Lord down. But he has never let me down—and that's really the secret of my faithfulness. I can be faithful to him because he upholds me, strengthens me, forgives me—and promises me a happy and secure future. How can I not be faithful to an ever-faithful God?

I have set the Lord always before me.
Because he is at my right hand, I will not be shaken....
Therefore my heart is glad and my tongue rejoices;
my body also will rest secure....
You have made known to me the path of life;
You will fill me with joy in your presence.

PSALM 16:8-11 NIV

MOLDED BY THE *Master*

When our son, Brad, was in high school, he took several pottery classes. In fact, he became quite an expert potter, and a number of his handcrafted pots and vases still decorate our house. I was always amazed at how Brad could take an ugly ball of clay and form it into a beautiful, useful object. Many times the first molding didn't come out the way he'd envisioned, but when that happened he'd just smash the whole thing back into a ball and start over. Brad knew, in his mind, what kind of end product he wanted, and he wasn't going to quit until he got it right.

That's the picture I get when I read in Scripture that God is a Potter and that you and I are clay in his hands. God knows what he's doing; he has a master plan for us. And he is molding my piece of clay into his image, not into my idea of what *I* want to be. It gives me great comfort to know I am being formed by the Master's hand.

> *O Lord, you are our Father. We are the clay and you are the Potter. We are all formed by your hand.*
>
> ISAIAH 64:8 TLB

Always

"If the Bible says it, I believe it." That's a good slogan to live by—as long as we go beyond just believing with our minds to obeying in our lives. The Bible means what it says, and that's important to keep in mind when we read 1 Thessalonians 5:16, which tells us to *always* be joyful, *always* keep praying, *always* be thankful.

Now, most of us manage to be joyful, to pray, to be thankful at least sometimes. But always? That's tough—but when God says always, he means always! For God's people, joy, prayer, and thanksgiving are supposed to be a constant. We are supposed to stay simple and pure before the Lord and live in a constant atmosphere of joy and prayer and thanksgiving. When that's true, we not only live in the full flow of God's blessing, but we reflect those blessings out into the world around us.

We can't do it without God's help, of course. But that's the heart of the Good News: he's also with us *always*.

> *Always be joyful. Always keep on praying. No matter what happens, always be thankful, for this is God's will for you who belong to Christ Jesus.*
>
> 1 THESSALONIANS 5:16-18 TLB

Abundant *Everything*

The dictionary defines *abundance* as having more than enough, having a great supply. And wouldn't life be wonderful if we always had an abundance of those things that make up the good life: health, wealth, success, happiness? A few more cars, a couple of vacation homes, a bigger church budget, another cabinet of teacups, some more beautiful grandkids? I certainly wouldn't mind!

But the abundance that God has promised us is better than any of those things! He's promised us abundance in the big three: mercy, peace, and love! If we're living in him, obeying him, our lives will overflow with these life-giving qualities.

Mercy, peace and love be yours in abundance.

JUDE 2 NIV

But what if we're feeling shortages in the mercy, peace, and love departments? We can usually look in the mirror and see who's at fault. God gives us what he promises, but we need to do it his way. And in order to have these qualities in abundance, we must first give them away to others. It's the way God does things: the more we give, the more we get.

WATER FOR *Life*

*H*ealth experts disagree about many things, but they all agree a hundred percent that drinking water is essential to health. It replenishes tissues, lubricates digestion, washes toxins out of the body. We just can't be healthy if we aren't "hydrated."

The experts also warn that if we wait to drink until we are thirsty, then we have probably waited too long to get the full benefit. It's important to drink plenty of water *before* we feel the call of thirst.

The Spirit and the bride say, "Come." Let each one who hears them say the same, "Come." Let the thirsty one come— anyone who wants to; let him come and drink the Water of Life without charge.

REVELATION 22:17 TLB

And the same is true of the living water Jesus offers. We shouldn't wait until our souls are dry and parched before coming to him. In fact, if we wait too long, we may lose our desire for "living water."

So if you hear the Holy Spirit calling you to come, don't wait. Come drink while you still hear his call. And keep on coming, even when you don't feel "thirsty!"

His water is free, and it doesn't come in plastic bottles!

A Lesson in a Time of *Testing*

*Y*es, Lord, I prayed to learn patience, but did you have to take me so literally? Was it really necessary for me to go through all this pain and suffering—all these examinations, hospital visits, blood transfusions, CAT scans, and all the other inconveniences that go with cancer treatments? I was ready for some little pop quizzes; I didn't really want the final exam!

Cross-examine me, O Lord, and see that this is so; test my motives and affections too. For I have taken your lovingkindness and your truth as my ideas.

PSALM 26:2-3 TLB

This experience with cancer has indeed been the hardest test of my life, and at times I have wondered if I'm up to it. Yet even in the midst of all the difficulties, I can see a little of what the Lord is doing in my life. For one thing, the ordeal of cancer treatment has forced me to examine my inmost heart—what I truly believe, what I care about, what I want to stand for. And my "motives and affections" have withstood the examination! During this time of testing I have been given the gift of reconfirming that God's ideas really are my ideas, and that I want to walk in faithfulness to him.

Now, if I can just get to patience a little faster....

Protected AND DELIVERED

*D*id you ever build a clubhouse or a fort as a child? Did you ever cover a table with blankets and crawl inside to a safe, cozy nest? That's what Psalm 34 reminds me of. The word *encampment* denotes making a camp or a fortress for protection—and that's what the Lord has done for me. I can feel it! Truly the Lord has given me my own special angel who wraps loving arms around me and delivers (or rescues) me from all harm. Even in my pain

> *The angel of the Lord encamps around those who fear him, and he delivers them.*
>
> PSALM 34:7 NIV

and fear I can feel the protection of loving prayers and vigilant love.

So I stand on this promise that no matter what happens, all's well. I believe the Lord will deliver me from my current danger in his time and in his way and that in the meantime he's keeping a close watch to keep me safe.

I continually feel his presence. He is always near.

GOD'S LOVING *Discipline*

This hurts me more than it hurts you." How many times have I spoken those words when disciplining my children—and later my grandchildren? And they were true—although the child receiving the discipline had a hard time understanding. It was only because I had such love for those little ones that I would take the trouble to teach and correct them.

And it is only because of God's great love that we are disciplined as well. He has

Do not despise the LORD's discipline
And do not resent his rebuke,
Because the LORD disciplines those he loves.

PROVERBS 3:11,12 NIV

created some basic laws of life; if we break them we will experience his correction. And it's not pleasant—nobody really likes to be disciplined. But being a parent gives me a little perspective—so I thank God that he loves me so much he wants me to grow and be the best I can be.

ENCOURAGING *Words*

Never in my life have I enjoyed reading God's Word as much as in the last two years. I'm not reading to take notes or preparing for a seminar; I'm just taking in the sweet words of the literature. Verse after verse has brought me such encouragement.

I especially appreciate those passages brought to my attention by loving friends who send me cards and letters. So many of these day-brighteners include a reference to a passage that has had meaning to the sender's life. As I read and meditate on these precious words, my soul is refreshed with a fresh sense of God's promises and faithfulness. Even familiar passages take on new meaning, and I enjoy them as never before. I've even started writing names and dates in the margins of my Bible besides certain special passages. That way, I will always have a record of when this reading was brought to my attention and who cared enough to share it with me.

For everything that was written in the past was written to teach us, so that through endurance and the encouragement of the Scriptures we might have hope.

ROMANS 15:4 NIV

SINGING FOR *Joy*

I don't know about you, but my heart overflows whenever I sing praises to the Lord. In church, the music often touches my heart and soul more deeply than the sermon or the prayers, and singing along with the congregation lets me praise the Lord and worship him out loud. At home, I love to sing along with the Christian music on the radio and CD player. The songs give me words and tunes that help express my need for God and my thankfulness for all

For the LORD takes delight in his people;
he crowns the humble with salvation.
Let the saints rejoice in his honor
and sing for joy on their beds.

PSALM 149:4,5 NIV

that he has done for me.

Now, I'll never be a recording artist or even a soloist in the church choir. But I know the Lord made my voice, and I know that he takes delight whenever he hears me singing his praise—even (or especially) when the singing comes through tears of gladness or sorrow. What a blessing to be able to open my mouth in his honor!

THE SECRET OF *Real* PEACE

"Blessed are the peacemakers," said Jesus in his Sermon on the Mount. And something deep inside all of us yearns for a world of peace and harmony. We are so very exhausted by all the conflicts we witness or hear about in this life. My television set screams out each day of a new horror in the world. Sometimes it seems as if the more we search for peace the less we experience it!

But God doesn't ever tell us to do something without helping us do it—and that's exactly the promise we find in this verse from Romans: God makes it possible for us to be peacemakers. The same God who gives us

May God who gives patience, steadiness, and encouragement help you to live in complete harmony with each other.

ROMANS 15:5 TLB

patience, steadiness, and encouragement also provides us the strength we need to live in harmony with each other.

No, we cannot save the world, but we can be an influence to those who we meet. With God's help, we can be instruments of his peace.

25

$\mathcal{G}$iving AND GETTING

$\mathcal{T}$here's more to living in the Lord's strength than just "soaking" in Scripture and prayer. The actual process of becoming strong and beautiful takes a bit more energy. It's a matter of doing what we think God wants us to do, trusting that we will be given the strength and guidance we need when we need it.

It is more blessed to give than to receive.

ACTS 20:35 NASB

The modern world says, "Give to me first, then I will give back to you." But the approach of Scripture is just the opposite. We're not supposed to just sit back and wait for others to give, but to be proactive and give first, with no expectations. No expectations, that is, except that in the act of giving we'll somehow receive God's blessing—and his blessings are always more wonderful than we ever anticipated!

A Job for *You*

One of God's most important promises is that each of us has important work to do—work that is instrumental in bringing about his kingdom. In fact, one of the most important tasks in life is to discover what we're supposed to be doing for him.

How do we do that? Through prayer, of course—and searching the Scriptures and seeking advice from wise counselors. But it also helps just to look around and ask, "How can I be of service?" When you do that, you're bound to discover a job you can do for Christ.

It might involve a big, high-profile challenge—or an ordinary, menial task. But even a humble chore, when done in Jesus' name, can be a graceful dance of love. Martin Luther once said that "a man can milk a cow to the glory of God." And that's the real point—to be willing to do what the Lord asks and to dedicate *all* our work to him. If we do that, we can trust him to guide us to the tasks he's set aside especially for us.

> *For we are God's workmanship, created in Christ Jesus to do good works, which God prepared in advance for us to do.*
>
> EPHESIANS 2:10 NIV

WHAT We CAN DO

God doesn't expect us to be strong, just obedient. We have to follow up on the little nudges and the big messages he sends us in our quiet times. We have to step forward, trusting that the Lord who gave the orders will also provide the strength to carry them out.

I'm constantly amazed at the way God uses ordinary people to shed his light to a hurting world—people like me and like you. Even our halting words and hesitant actions, if done in love and obedience, can yield big results. We can bring peace to a hurting person. We can bring light to people who are lost and confused. All we have to do is take the risk and reach out. You can trust our loving, tender God to take it from there.

> *All this will be because the mercy of our God is very tender, and heaven's dawn is about to break upon us, to give light to those who sit in darkness and death's shadow, and to guide us to the path of peace.*
>
> LUKE 1:78,79 TLB

Everything to the *Lord*

The Lord asks us to give him the whole of our lives, from living to dying. Sometimes that feels like a blessed relief, sometimes a painful sacrifice—often a mixture of the two. And most of us have to do it again and again, because we have this annoying tendency to keep snatching back the reins and trying to run things ourselves—as if we couldn't trust the Lord of the Universe, the Creator of all things, the Redeemer of our souls, to take care of our lives as well!

For not one of us lives for himself, and not one dies for himself; for if we live, we live for the Lord, or if we die, we die for the Lord; therefore whether we live or die, we are the Lord's.

ROMANS 14:7,8 NASB

The Bible says the whole reason we're here is to know, love, and serve God—and that only comes through giving ourselves to him. Here's how it works: First, we give him all of ourselves. Then he fills us with all we could ever want of him. And then, as a bonus, he gives us back ourselves as well. What a bargain! What a Lord!

THAT *Much!*

The most incredible aspect of salvation is that I, personally, have a part in God's story. You do, too. And our part is, basically, to trust him, to let him work in our lives and to change us and guide us. I have never regretted trusting my life to God—again and again, in the face of doubt and despair, he has proved trustworthy. I have often regretted *not* trusting him, though—for my own plans and strategies have often backfired.

Trusting comes easier when we get it through our heads just how deeply God loves and cares for each one of us—and this Scripture promise spells it out in beautiful detail. He loves us more tenderly than a woman loves her tiny infant. He loves us so much he can never forget us. He's even written our names on his very being, so we'll be part of him forever. That's love we can trust!

Can a woman forget her nursing child
And have no compassion on the son of her womb?
Even these may forget, but I will not forget you.
Behold, I have inscribed you on the palms of My hands.

ISAIAH 49:15,16 NASB

Blessings in the *Word*

Quiet times can happen any-where, as long as you are able to pull away, to shut a door, to put space between you and the ordinary demands of your day. Each day I delight in meeting God so we can communicate together. I get such great inspiration and encour-agement from these times together. Without these precious moments, my life would be a mess.

Particularly of late, during my quiet times, the Lord has nudged me toward Scripture that gives me com-fort and assurance so that I can take the next step forward. I wake in the morning and fall asleep at night with his words. The more time I spend in the Word, the more I am aware of the blessings it brings me.

Teach me, O Lord, the way of Thy statutes,
And I shall observe it to the end.
Give me understanding, that I may observe Thy law,
And keep it with all my heart.
Make me walk in the path of Thy commandments,
For I delight in it.

PSALM 119:33-35, NASB

Comfort
FOR DARK NIGHTS

*H*eavenly Father, in the past two years I have walked so many times in the dark valley of pain and fear and death—but even in my darkest hour you have been my comfort. Without your loving arms' being wrapped around me, I truly could not have survived! You have sent your living servants to hold my hands, rub my feet, bring bouquets of flowers and family

*Even though I walk through the valley
    of the shadow of death,
I fear no evil; for Thou art with me;
Thy rod and Thy staff, they comfort me.*

PSALM 23:4 NASB

photos to brighten my room, even clean my house. You have spoken to me through the soothing and uplifting music of a Christian radio station. You have given me encouraging words through Scripture. And sometimes, when I gave in to resentment and self-pity, you have gently admonished me, disciplining me back toward the comforting awareness of your presence.

You have done all this for me when I was at my lowest point. Why should I be afraid of any future evil? I know you can handle it!

Lightening
OUR LOADS

We become strong women of God when we offer him our burdens and weaknesses and ask him in all humility to lighten our loads and give us his strength. What an incredible thought: The power that runs the universe is available to us if we are humble enough to accept it!

So why do we keep on staggering under our loads of guilt, resentment, stress, and worry? Why do we keep obsessing over how much we have to do? Usually it's our own stubborn pride that keeps us over-loaded. We'd rather break our backs doing it our way than admit our load's too heavy—or that we might be carrying a burden that was never meant for us.

It's really silly when you think about it! How much simpler just to swallow our pride and listen to what God is saying. He's got work for us to do—important work. But it's never more than we can handle with his help.

Come to Me, all you who labor and are heavy laden, and I will give you rest. Take My yoke upon you and learn from Me, for I am gentle and lowly in heart, and you will find rest for your souls. For My yoke is easy and My burden is light.

MATTHEW 11:28–30 NKJV

MORE THAN *Just Words*

Words, words, words! Sometimes to be honest, that's what the Bible seemed like to me. Sometimes it was confusing or hard to understand. Sometimes—especially when life was going well—I would read through whole passages without any sense of what they really meant.

But during the tough times, the times when my life began to crumble, I found that the words of Scripture really came to life!

For I am persuaded that neither death nor life, nor angels nor principalities nor powers, nor things present nor things to come, nor height nor depth, nor any other created thing, shall be able to separate us from the love of God which is in Christ Jesus our Lord.

ROMANS 8:38,39 NKJV

Scriptures I had read and memorized were leaping to my mind and helping me cope. Familiar passages suddenly took on new depth of meaning.

And what wonderful comfort the familiar words of Romans 8 have held for me in light of my own troubles. They remind me that the Lord is with me in my pain, but he also is greater than pain, greater than fear, greater even than death.

Nothing can separate me from God's love—and that's more than just words! That's rock-solid, dependable, life-giving truth.

THE PURPOSE OF *Prayer*

*P*rayer can be a form of service in itself, but it also increases our capacity and desire to serve in other ways. When we are coming to the Lord regularly in prayer, we are growing in compassion, in understanding, and in our willingness to serve.

When we find our problems are greater than we are able to handle, we often turn to prayer more fervently. We read books, listen to tapes, talk to friends—trying to unravel this mystery of how it works. What should I pray for? How can my petitions be answered? What is the purpose of it all?

After much searching I have come to believe that the *first* purpose of prayer is to bring us alongside God's will. We're not asking for his support of our plans—but we're asking to be part of his plans. How it all works is still a mystery. But it *does* work…and it is changing my life with every hour I spend in prayer!

Now this is the confidence that we have in Him, that if we ask anything according to His will, He hears us. And if we know that He hears us, whatever we ask, we know that we have the petitions that we have asked of Him.

1 JOHN 5:14,15 NKJV

THE BASICS OF *Grace*

I've discovered one surefire way to wear myself out—trying to work myself into God's good graces. What a futile effort! I could work and work until the end of eternity and still not be able to deserve God's love or rate forgiveness for my sins. Nothing I have done, can do, or will do *is* enough.

But God is enough! What Christ did on the cross was enough. And because of that, the process of being made right with God works so simply and beautifully. I simply hold up my life—all of it—to my loving, giving heavenly Father. I trust him with who I am. And then, in his mercy, he makes me into something better. He cleanses me of the old, the impure, the bitter. Then he fills me with the living water of forgiveness, quietness, encouragement, trust, communion, strength, and thanksgiving. Through the miracle of grace, I am truly saved from myself.

Because of his great love for us, God, who is rich in mercy, made us alive with Christ even when we were dead in transgressions.... For it is by grace you have been saved, through faith—and this not from yourselves, it is the gift of God—not by works, so that no one can boast.

EPHESIANS 2:4, 8,9 NIV

THE SHADE UNDER *His Wings*

As a young child, I loved to look down at the sidewalk on a bright sunny day and see the shadows of the clouds and planes overhead. Since I lived in a hot area, I always liked the big clouds because they blocked out the hot sun rays and gave some relief from the high temperatures. So I can just imagine what kind of shadow God's wings would cast. I know that it would be much larger than that of a sparrow, even larger than an American bald eagle or even a California condor. I can just feel that cool shade. And I'm so glad I can relax in the cool shadow of his mighty wings.

How precious is Your lovingkindness, O God!
Therefore the children of men put their trust
under the shadow of Your wings.

PSALM 36:7 NKJV

ETERNALLY *Bright*

*Invariably, after our grand-children have visited us for the weekend, none of our flashlights work. All the batteries are drained from all the hours spent searching attic and garage, exploring the outdoors by night, and investigating secret hiding places. Children are just fascinated by a beam of light in the darkness. And how disappointed they are when the batteries finally burn low and the light falters.

But the truth is that all lights here on earth eventually falter. Lightbulbs burn out. Power grids black out. Daylight turns to darkness as the earth turns—and one day, we're told, even the dependable sun will flicker out.

What a contrast to the eternal brightness of God's kingdom, which shines now as a light in the darkness and one day will surround us as ever-lasting light! God's batteries are always charged up. They never go out.

> *The sun will no more be your light by day,*
> *nor will the brightness of the moon shine on you,*
> *for the LORD will be your everlasting light,*
> *and your God will be your glory.*
> *Your sun will never set again,*
> *and your moon will wane no more;*
> *the LORD will be your everlasting light,*
> *and your days of sorrow will end.*
>
> ISAIAH 60:19,20 NIV

THE *Joyful* CREATION

One of the great joys of summer is vacation time with the family—and one of our favorite memory makers was a recent trip to Idaho. This state abounds with unspoiled beauty—majestic mountains, sparkling rivers, lush vegetation. Many places, in fact, look much as they did hundred of years ago. We had a wonderful time—fishing and hiking, roasting wieners over a crackling fire, and camping out under the wide sky. At night, as the sky darkened and the stars began to dance, we could literally hear God's creation shouting with joy and clapping her hands. (It sounded like lapping water, singing breezes, chirping insects, and clean, deep silence.)

Since then, wherever I am, I try to listen more carefully to the joyful voices of creation all around me—a dancing sea breeze, a purring cat, a rustling clump of desert grass. All these sounds bless me—they remind me of just how good the Creator is, and they inspire me to sing along!

For you will go out with joy,
And be led forth with peace;
The mountains and the hills will break forth into
shouts of joy before you,
And all the trees of the field will clap their hands.

ISAIAH 55:12 NASB

THE HUMBLE WILL BE *Exalted*

A few years ago I had the opportunity to attend the forty-year reunion of my high-school class. I could hardly wait to reacquaint myself with the sports heroes, the cheerleaders, the homecoming queens, and my fellow student-body officers.

Well, it was fun to see all those people I knew so long ago. But I was shocked to see how many of the most popular, well-known people in my class had fallen on difficult times. At the same time, many of those who were lesser known in high school had really made something of themselves. It was exciting to see how many of the humble had been exalted in due time.

I realized clearly at that reunion that not only does our high school ranking not determine our ranking years later—but that we shouldn't take any kind of earthly ranking too seriously. Regardless of what others think of us, we are all in God's hands—and he cares for us, no matter how well known and popular we are.

> *Therefore humble yourselves under the mighty hand of God, that He may exalt you in due time, casting all your care upon Him, for He cares for you.*
>
> 1 PETER 5:6,7 NKJV

THE BLESSING OF A *Life*

I am so thankful that my mother stood up to my father and said she would have no more abortions—she had already had two previous ones to please him.

My frame was not hidden from you when I was made in the secret place. When I was woven together in the depths of the earth, your eyes saw my unformed body. All the days ordained for me were written in your book before one of them came to be.

PSALM 139:15,16 NIV

I would accept Jesus as my Messiah and my personal savior. Little did my family realize that my name was long ago written in His book.

Life is so precious! We need to give every child in a mother's womb the opportunity to grow into the person that God has planned for him or her from the very beginning.

Because of her bravery I was able to be born and to fulfill the life that God had for me. Little did I know when I was conceived in my Jewish mother's womb that many years later

MEANT TO BE *Shared*

When the Lord fills our cup, he fills it to be used. He intends for us to fill the cups of others the best way we know how. And when we do, the sweetness of his love and peace flows from cup...to cup...to cup...to cup. I would never have guessed, when I was a young wife many years ago, that one day I would write books and conduct large seminars telling women how to get organized, how to care for a home, how to love their families, and live as a woman of God. You see, I just had a high school education, and I didn't feel adequate to tell anyone what to do!

But little by little, some other women started to recognize my gifts for organization and for speaking. They began to affirm my worthiness, and some even invited me to share what I knew with their women's groups. Over the years, as I made use of my gifts to administer God's grace to others, I've felt his grace overflow in my own life as well.

Each one should use whatever gift he has received to serve others, faithfully administering God's grace in its various forms.

1 PETER 4:10 NIV

LESSONS FOR *Rising*

*Arise, shine, for your light has come,
and the glory of the LORD rises upon you…
Then you will look and be radiant,
your heart will throb and swell with joy.*

ISAIAH 60:1,5 NIV

What's the best way to arise so that you truly shine? Take a little time to start the day right, preparing yourself to greet the world.

Here's a routine that helps me. First get out of bed and make the bed (unless your husband is still in it!). Take a minute to stretch and touch your toes. Then shower or at least wash your face and teeth, put a little paint "on the barn," and dress in appropriate attire for the day. Then sit down in the quiet of the morning and spend a little time with God before the hectic morning really starts. Ask God to help your heart throb and swell with joy—the whole day long.

The Lord has given you the desire to start a new day with a positive attitude—and following a positive routine really helps. You are still a new person; ready to meet the challenges of a new day. Even through your yawns, you are beginning to reflect the radiance from the light of the Lord.

THE MODEL *Woman*

*O*h Lord, where can I go to find models for the kind of woman I want to be—the kind of woman you had in mind when you created me? I look at television, and I can't find her there. I look in magazines, and she's certainly not there. I even switch on the radio and I can't hear her. But here in the pages of Scripture I see her depicted beautifully. Here is a picture of a woman I can be proud to be.

Strength and honor are her clothing;
She shall rejoice in time to come.
She opens her mouth with wisdom;
And on her tongue is the law of kindness.

PROVERBS 31:25,26 NKJV

I want to be a virtuous woman. I want strength and honor. I want a tongue that utters wisdom and kindness. And only with your help, Lord, can I be that kind of woman. Please guard my mouth from the evils of gossip, hatred, and character assassination. Please show me how to be disciplined and self-controlled and live with integrity. Help me be the kind of woman I can look up to, the kind who pleases you.

God CAN DO ANYTHING!

J claim this promise for myself—that God is able to heal me of my illness and that he will heal me according to his purposes. One way or another, I believe a miracle of healing is being accomplished in my life, and I thank God he is able to accomplish this.

I know that my God is above all that is in this world, and that he owns everything. The cattle on a thousand hills are his, and he knows the number of sand pebbles on all the beaches. He has created all the stars, and he knows each of them by their name, and he made and knows me, too. He is an omnipotent helper, and he gives me an abundance of strength. I look forward with confidence to the day of my full recovery on this earth.

> *But for you who revere my name, the sun of righteousness will rise with healing in its wings. And you will go out and leap like calves released from the stall.*
>
> MALACHI 4:2 NIV

The Greatest *Gift*

*J*ohn 3:16 contains the greatest promise in the Scriptures. Without it, all the rest would be meaningless. By the very act of sacrificing his Son, God gave me a way to be with him forever and forever. I want to grasp this concept and to trust my everyday to living out its truth. Lord, I know that I'm living out eternity now! I don't have to wait until I die to be with you, because today is part of that period of time when we'll be together.

Your gift of eternal salvation is the greatest gift that one person can give another. Thank you for what you have done for me. Help me live so that everything I do reflects my love and appreciation for your great gift.

For God so loved the world that He gave His only begotten Son, that whoever believes in Him should not perish, but have eternal life.

JOHN 3:16 NASB

Working for God

In the days of old, a man or woman's work was perceived as God's blessing; people would do their work "as unto the Lord." In studying history we find the great musicians, sculptors, painters, craftsmen all creating works reflecting their love for God.

Today, we seem to have lost that tremendous concept. Many of us today look upon work as a penalty or a burden. We struggle to drag ourselves out of bed in the morning to go to that boring job or begin on the drudgery of housework. We live for the weekend instead of appreciating the gift of our daily tasks.

I think we would be a lot happier—and much better workers—if we recaptured that idea that our work, our wealth, and our possessions are all gifts from God, and we can thank him by doing our very best. As Christians we should be the best workers on our street or in our company.

When God gives any man wealth and possessions, and enables him to enjoy them, to accept his lot and be happy in his work—this is a gift of God.

ECCLESIASTES 5:19 NIV

THE BLESSING OF A *Smile*

Wherever I go, a smile is the common denominator for happiness. I have never turned down a smile sent in my direction, nor have I become angry to anyone who smiles back at me. To me, a smile is a blessing one person can give another. It costs the giver very little, and the receiver takes away a beautiful, unexpected gift. You'll never know when your smile is the only smile a person will receive that day.

You've probably heard that it takes more muscles to frown than to smile. That's true—but a smiling does take some effort. It takes wisdom enough to notice another person and choose to connect with him or her, to share a little something from the heart. A smile might not be returned— but it's never wasted. Shared blessings never are.

Wisdom makes one's face shine, and the hardness of one's countenance is changed.

ECCLESIASTES 8:1 NRSV

THE WAY TO *Bless* ONE ANOTHER

I am so thankful for all of my kind and compassionate friends. The outpouring of self-giving love I have experienced the past few years has absolutely astonished me. Cards, letters, candies, flowers, faxes all have flowed from friends and family and even from those who know me only from my books and seminars. I have learned so much about love and caring from these people who have shown me amazing kindness and compassion.

But it is the people who have forgiven me my faults and failings who leave me really humble—friends and family who sometimes become the target of my cross

Be kind and compassionate to one another, forgiving each other, just as in Christ God forgave you.

EPHESIANS 4:32 NIV

moods or critical spirit, planners of meetings I have had to cancel, phone friends who understand unreturned calls, gracious acquaintances who answer my apologies with smiling good grace. It is the forgiveness of others that reminds me of how much my heavenly Father forgives me— and how important it is for me to cultivate the art of forgiveness in my own heart. Forgiveness works at a soul level, and it eventually changes everything— beginning with the heart of the forgiver.

49

THE PROMISE OF *Spring*

For the winter is past, the rain is over and gone. The flowers are springing up and the time of the singing of birds has come. Yes, spring is here.

SONG OF SOLOMON 2:11,12 TLB

I so look forward to getting past the winter and rains. It seems like its been so long since I've seen the budding of the spring flowers or heard the chirping of a new song-bird. I realize there are various seasons of one's life, and I can assure you that these last few months have not been easy on me or my family and friends. These people I love have been wonderful during this winter season of my life; they have come alongside and assured me that spring will come.

I believe them, and I can't wait. Come on spring! I can't wait for you to arrive.

A HOME THAT *Smiles*

There is an old southern saying which goes, "If Mama Ain't Happy, Ain't Nobody Happy!" And it's true. The woman of the house is almost always the one who sets the "temperature" of the home—her mood is catching to everyone else in the family. If she cultivates a joyous, cheerful spirit, that spirit will spread throughout the family—and practically light up the home.

How do you go about cultivating a happy spirit? Not by being fake or syrupy, but by setting aside time to focus on God's love. Your joy in life has to come as a reflection of the love you absorb from him during your quiet time. If you are wrestling with painful issues—and most of us do, from time to time—talk it out with caring friends, seek counseling if you need it, pour out your heart in a journal and in your prayers. But when your husband or your children come home, do what you can to put a smile in your heart and on your face. You'll feel better, and so will everyone else!

Their children will see it and be joyful;
Their hearts will rejoice in the Lord.

ZECHARIAH 10:7 NIV

YOUR *Needs* WILL BE MET

As of today I have lived through 22,065 days, and every day I have found the promise of Luke 12:30 to be true in my life. I've had my ups and downs, but always God has provided my needs. As a little girl with an alcoholic, sometimes violent father, I was protected. As a teenager living with my single-parent mom in the little three-room apartment behind our dress store, I never went hungry. Money was often tight, but I can't remember not having clothes for school, a roof over our head, a loving family, or caring friends. As newlyweds in a tiny apartment, Bob and I often struggled to make ends meet, but still there was always enough.

Now, during my adult years, the Lord has graciously blessed me above all my expectations—both materially and spiritually. He truly is a provider of all good things.

Your heavenly Father knows your needs. He will always give you all you need from day to day.

LUKE 12:30,31 TLB

THE KEY TO *Success*

Successful people do what unsuccessful people aren't willing to do. And the book of Joshua makes the key to success very clear: We are not to let God's Word depart from our mouths! That means that we do more than just flip through the Bible occasionally or even set aside fifteen minutes a day for Scripture reading. Instead, we are to think and ponder God's Word twenty-four hours a day! Even when we aren't actually reading, what we've read is at the back of our minds. And when we do that, God's Word becomes part of us—it changes how we think, how we relate to others, even how we define success!

During the past two difficult years, I've learned first-hand what a difference meditating on God's precious book can make. Never have I felt his comfort and assurances like I have in this season of my life—even though I have faced some of my toughest challenges. Because of my growing love for God's Word, I truly consider myself successful and prosperous. No one could desire more.

> *Do not let this Book of the Law depart from your mouth; meditate on it day and night, so that you may be careful to do everything written in it. Then you will be prosperous and successful.*
>
> JOSHUA 1:8 NIV

Blessings
Too Many To Count

Since I was raised in a Jewish home, I never learned any Christian hymns. Thus I was a grownup before I learned the one that goes, "Count your blessings, name them one by one…." But I loved this idea of thinking about numbering blessings and literally calling the name of each one. Now, whenever I become despondent or discouraged, all I have to do is start listing what God has done for me— both heaven's blessings such as God's love and Christ's sacrifice and earthly joys such as visits from my grandchildren or beautiful days at the beach. Before I know it, my attitude has shifted to one of overwhelmed thankfulness for all that God has given me.

If you're feeling a little bit down, I heartily recommend this practice of counting blessings. Just take a sheet of paper and divide it down the middle with a line. At the head of one column write "Heavenly Blessings," and for the other write "Human Joys." Start filling your paper with every blessing you can think of—and watch your attitude improve.

May the Lord continually bless you with heaven's blessings as well as with human joys.

PSALM 128:5 TLB

NOTHING'S TOO HARD FOR *God*

*D*ear Lord, I don't know why I even try to understand you with my small brain. You are so much greater than I am. I stand in awe when I journey to the mountains, the desert, the beach and see all of your creations. When I feel the rumble of earthquakes here in California or witness on the news the mighty forces of hurricanes and tornadoes, I can't comprehend the power of your creation. You truly are awesome, and I know you can do anything!

But even though I can't understand you, I do trust you to do what you have promised. I pray that your will might be done in my life and that I can hear and accept your direction for my life. And if it fits your plan, I ask for added days to my life—I know you can do that, too—and thank you for granting me such favor.

Ah, Lord God! Behold, You have made the heavens and the earth by Your great power and outstretched arm. There is nothing too hard for You.

JEREMIAH 32:17 NKJV

THE *Story*
CREATION TELLS

*D*o you want evidence that God is at work in the universe? Just look around at the amazing things he has created! Green trees dancing in the breeze. Thunderclouds piling high on summer afternoons. A peaceful full moon. All these have a story to tell—the story of God's greatness.

As we get away from the city lights we are able to get an even better view of the mighty Creator in action. Ocean waves, desert sunrises, mountain streams, star-filled skies— all tell us so much about his greatness. Think of what ancient people and early explorers must have

The heavens declare the glory of God;
the skies proclaim the work of his hands.
Day after day they pour forth speech;
night after night they display knowledge.

PSALM 19:1,2 NIV

seen each night as the sun set and the darkness of the evening brought forth the sights and sounds of the unspoiled universe!

But even in the city, the works of God's creation shout their praise to him. There is no show on earth as awesome as the smallest display of what God has made—including human beings! Surely we, too, should shout his praise!

A PROMISE OF *Light*

of God—and what he's here for—to show us how to live, and to take care of our sinful condition once and for all. We need to pay attention to that kind of authority. We need to listen to what Jesus has to say and obey it. And what Jesus says over and over, in one way or another, is: "Follow me. I'll light your path and show you the way."

Dear Lord, you are my only dependable and authoritative guide—truly the light of my world. Teach me to follow you more trustingly, more courageously, more completely.

As long as I am in the world, I am the light of the world.

JOHN 9:5 NKJV

*L*isten to the authority that lies behind Jesus' words in the biblical promise! It's the confident authority of One who knows exactly who he is—the Son

No More!

Who else can give us a promise like the one found in Revelation 21? It's a mouth-watering picture of what life in eternity with him will be like.

Just think of a life with no more tears … no more death … no more sorrow … no more crying … no more pain! No more of the familiar, unavoidable pain of being human. It will all disappear forever.

He will wipe away all tears from their eyes, and there shall be no more death, nor sorrow, nor crying, nor pain. All of that has gone forever.

REVELATION 21:4 TLB

Hard to imagine, isn't it? We live in a fallen and depraved world which creates an abundance of dysfunctions in our lives. Pain and unhappiness are familiar to all of us, no matter what our position in life might be. Some have illness. Some have money troubles. Some agonize over disrupted relationships.

But it won't be like that for those who have followed Christ—we have God's promise on that. Someday all our pain will all be wiped away, never to be experienced again. I look forward with great anticipation to that heavenly event. Hope you are there with me.

Loosing the *Chains*

Have you ever had times when you felt ineffective for the Lord, when your prayer life just seemed to be on hold? "What's the matter?" you may ask. When I've asked that question, the answers sometime surprise me!

I remember an awful time in my life when my daughter had left her husband. I was so upset with her and worried about her children! And I prayed and prayed that there would be healing in that family. But months passed, and nothing seemed to change. Finally I started complaining to God, asking him why he wasn't answering my prayers. And his still, small voice gave me an unexpected answer: I was to ask my daughter for forgiveness.

What? Me ask *her* forgiveness? She was the one who caused all this the trouble! But I wanted to obey God, so I went to her and apologized for my resentment and anger. And only then did the healing begin—for my pain, for hers, for our relationships. It couldn't happen until I loosened the chains of blame and resentment that were getting in the way of God's work!

> Loose the chains of injustice
> and untie the cords of the yoke....
> Then your light will break forth like the dawn,
> and your healing will quickly appear.
>
> ISAIAH 58:6,8 NIV

A DEPENDABLE *Promise*

Where do I turn when my world has been turned upside down and I can't get up from this pile I'm under? The world offers a lot of options, but none of them give a satisfying or lasting solution to my problems. The Scriptures do, though. The Bible is full of promises and guarantees for those of us who know the Lord by name. His words echo in my ears when he states that because I love and trust him he will not only rescue me but even make me great. He goes on to assure me that he will answer me when I'm in trouble, that he will honor me, that I will have a full life with his salvation.

No other worldly solution offers that amount of assurance. No one else is ultimately dependable. The Lord of the Bible is one that I can trust with my eternity.

For the Lord says, "Because he loves me, I will rescue him; I will make him great because he trusts in my name. When he calls on me I will answer; I will be with him in trouble, and rescue him and honor him. I will satisfy him with a full life and give him my salvation."

PSALM 91:14–16 TLB

WHAT THE *Blood* CAN DO

*We all, like sheep, have gone astray,
each of us has turned to his own way;
and the LORD has laid on him
the iniquity of us all.*

ISAIAH 53:6 NIV

What can wash away my sin? Nothing but the blood of Jesus. What can make me whole again? Nothing but the blood of Jesus." I never heard that hymn until I was an adult—because I didn't become a Christian until I was sixteen years old. In fact, when I was first confronted by the claims of Jesus, I replied that I didn't need Christianity because I wasn't a sinner. I wasn't a criminal or a drunk. I was a good girl!

But then I was introduced to Isaiah 53: "We all have gone astray"—and I recognized myself. I did like to follow my own way, even if it led me astray and got me lost. Put that way, I was a sinner—a wandering sheep in need of being found.

Then I discovered there was only one thing that would take away this sin. That's right: "Nothing but the blood of Jesus!" I let the Lord find me—and began the lifelong process of letting him make me whole.

God Will Be Found

I don't know about your husband, but my Bob can't find anything in the kitchen without first calling out, "Emilie, where is the _____?" Invariably, I go to the cupboard and it's right there. It might be hiding behind the sugar canister or a can of corn. Or it might be there in plain view—he just didn't see it.

"You will seek me and find me when you seek me with all your heart. I will be found by you," declares the Lord.

JEREMIAH 29:13,14 NIV

I think God is like that sometimes. He's not that hard to find. He isn't stuck in some corner of the refrigerator or the back part of a dark pantry. He is out in the bright light of the day, and even in the darkness of night he's right there. His fingerprints are all over his creation, and his presence is as close as our breath. And yet, sometimes we have a hard time seeing what is right there in front of our faces.

But don't give up searching, even if God seems to be absent. The problem is with your seeing, not with his presence! The Word promises that if we search for God with all our hearts we *will* find him. He's been right here all the time!

Listening
FOR HIS VOICE

_A_gain and again, Scripture affirms the power of God's voice—yet sometimes I have had trouble hearing it or understanding what he is saying to me. When that happens, it's usually because I've been wandering away from him. I haven't been paying regular attention to his Word or spending time with him in daily prayer. I forget what his voice sounds like.

But the more time I spend in God's presence, the more familiar his voice becomes. I recognize his voice in sudden thoughts that are clearly not my own. I hear him speaking through words of Scripture that just seem to jump off the page or through another person's words that seem to ring with eternal authority.

If I am taking the time to stay close to the Lord, he _will_ speak to me. And when I do recognize my Shepherd's voice, I need to obey it. If I don't follow where he leads, chances are I'll drift off the path and have a harder time hearing him in the future.

My sheep hear My voice, and I know them, and they follow Me; and I give eternal life to them, and they shall never perish; and no one shall snatch them out of my hand.

JOHN 10:27,28 NASB

Always More to *Learn*

For more than forty years now, I have cried out, "Lord make me know Thy ways." I have read, studied, and prayed. I have tried to follow his paths and learn his truth. And yet, the more I have learned about God over these forty years, the more I realize how little I know! The God of the Bible is infinite and mysterious. He rarely does things the way I would do them. Often he surprises me with the way he works.

In a way, that's comforting. Would I really want a God who was completely understandable? If he weren't awesome and mysterious and

Make me know Thy ways, O Lord;
Teach me Thy paths.
Lead me in Thy truth and teach me,
For Thou art the God of my salvation;
For Thee I wait all the day.

PSALM 25:4,5 NASB

beyond understanding, would he even be God?

Besides, though I'll never completely understand God, I definitely know enough to trust him. Again and again he has shown me that his ways are better than my ways and that I always do better to follow his paths—learning more and more as I go along, and trusting him to show me more of himself as we travel on together.

THE SECRET OF *Success*

*I*f you're like me, you want to know how a project is going to turn out before you throw your heart and soul into it. *Will it be a success?* I wonder. *Will it be worth my while?*

But the truth is, it's all but impossible to know what the outcome of our efforts will be—especially when we're doing God's work. Success is not really our responsibility. We're just called to do what God asks us—witnessing for Him, helping those in need, living lives of integrity—and leave the outcome to him. Just as a farmer sows a seed and trusts the rain and sunshine to do the rest, we need to do our part and trust God with the results.

We may never know the outcome of our caring deeds or words of witness. Or we may have the joy and surprise of seeing what our "seeds" have yielded. (Hearing from people whose lives have been changed is one of the chief perks of my ministry.) Either way, our job is to be faithful and obedient. Our God will do the rest.

Cast your bread upon the waters,
for after many days you will find it again.

ECCLESIASTES 11:1 NIV

I'll Come Back for You

And if I go and prepare a place for you, I will come back and take you to be with me that you also may be where I am. You know the way to the place where I am going.

JOHN 14:3,4 NIV

My heart flutters when I take in the promise of John 14—just to think that someday (in his time) I will be with God forever. This passage makes it very clear that Christ is coming again to fetch those for whom he has prepared a glorious place. And this promise is good for anyone who has accepted him as Savior. If you know him as Lord, you know the way to eternal life.

To make sure you are going to make it, simply acknowledge your need as a sinner and invite him into your heart to forgive you. His Word says he will never drive out anyone who comes to him. Just tell him who you are and accept the gift he has to offer—the gift of a whole new life. Then, when Jesus returns again to claim his church, you'll be ready and waiting with ticket in hand. All aboard!

Becoming *New*

Therefore, if anyone is in Christ, he is a new creation; the old has gone, the new has come!

2 CORINTHIANS 5:17 NIV

It all began one evening many years ago. That was when I knelt beside my bed and asked Jesus to come into my life. I asked him to forgive me of all my sins—past, present and future—and to direct my paths from then on. And at that moment, this sixteen-year-old Jewish girl became a new creation in Christ. It was a quiet moment, with no bells or whistles, and yet I knew it had made a tremendous difference in my life. It was the beginning of a lifetime journey, learning what being a new person meant.

Today, as I look at my battered Bible with all its dog-eared pages, its underlined and highlighted passages, and its margin notes—including the names of people who have shared key passages with me—I almost feel as if I'm looking at a road map of my life as a new creation. Chills come over me as I realized how much has changed since that evening long ago—and how much remains the same. I became new in an instant, but it's taken me a lifetime to become the person I am today in Christ.

The Promise of *Prayer*

I've had friends apologize to me because they forgot to pray for me that day. But I'm not particularly worried about their mistake because I know that God knows their heart—and accepted the loving prayers their minds forgot to make.

God provides for us in so many ways without our even having to ask. And yet he wants us to ask. This seems to be very important to him—maybe it's the only way he can get us to talk to him! In fact, he has promised that he'll do whatever we ask in prayer. Surely we forfeit a lot of God's blessings because we will not act on this promise.

Well, I intend to take God at his word. For the past two years I've had thousands of prayer warriors petitioning God for my healing, and I have felt myself being carried by those prayers. I don't know how God will choose to answer those prayers and fill my needs—I'm banking on a miracle. But whatever the specific outcome on this side of heaven, I'm trusting that it will all be for my good...and his glory.

> *And whatever you ask in my name, that I will do, that the Father may be glorified in the Son.*
>
> JOHN 14:13 NKJV

GOOD NEWS FOR *Always*

But seek first his kingdom and his righteousness, and all these things will be given to you as well.

MATTHEW 6:33 NIV

This particular passage has been my family's theme verse for the past thirty years. It has served us well. When difficult decisions needed to be made, we always tried to ask ourselves, "Does what we are about to do help us seek God's kingdom and his righteousness?" If not, we just won't do it.

Having this verse as a benchmark has certainly helped us understand the will of God in our lives. For instance, we know that if the thought of giving away a certain possession is just too painful, that might be a sign that it's become too important in our lives. It might even be getting in the way of seeking God's kingdom—so something's got to give.

SIMPLE PROMISE OF *Salvation*

"How can I become a Christian?" Have you ever had anyone ask you this basic question? I just love it when a searching soul comes to me or writes me wanting to know how to be a follower of Jesus. I love to tell him or her how simple and wonderful it is.

There are really just two requirements, according to this New Testament promise: (1) a person must confess out loud that Jesus Christ is Lord—the Messiah, the Savior—and (2) that person must believe that God raised Jesus from the dead.

It doesn't stop there, of course. After confessing and believing, the new Christian has a whole new life in front of him or her. The surrendered Christian life can also be summed up in just a few words? There's trust, as in: "Trust in the Lord with all your heart…" (Proverbs 3:5 NIV) There's love, as in: "Love the Lord… with all your heart … and love your neighbor as yourself" (Mark 12:30 NIV). And there's tell, as in: "Go… tell them how much the Lord has done for you" (Mark 5:19 NIV).

It takes just a minute to learn those words. Living them out can take a lifetime—but what a wonderful life it will be!

> *If you confess with your mouth, "Jesus is Lord," and believe in your heart that God raised him from the dead, you will be saved.*
>
> ROMANS 10:9 NIV

Celebrating
HIS PRESENCE

Your quiet time is not a gift you give to God, but a gift God gives to you. Don't think of it as offering him your "quiet time." Simply offer him your time, yourself. He's the one who will provide the quiet spirit. Get in the habit of saying, "Good morning, Lord" and "Good evening, Lord." This practice will gives you joy in the morning and peace at night. Start and end each day with

Every morning tell him, "Thank you for your kindness," and every evening rejoice in all his faithfulness.

PSALM 92:2 TLB

some time of simply being with God. Wait a minute before bringing him all your petitions and concerns. First, remember and be thankful for the prayers he has answered in the past. And let all your praying be preceded by praise. We must remember that it's in the authority of Jesus' name that we can expect answers to our prayers. We can be courageous in our asking and confident in his answers. But first, we have the privilege of celebrating God's presence—for his very faithfulness is a promise and a blessing in one.

A Little *Appreciation*

When I talk with burned-out women at our seminars, their number-one complaint is that no one in the family appreciates them. They work very hard—shopping, cooking, cleaning, scrubbing, picking up, driving carpools, sharing their love with their families—and very seldom do they receive a thank-you. Seldom do they hear, "That was a good meal," "Thanks for washing and ironing my clothes," or "The house always looks so good." Rarely is there applause or acclaim. They feel ignored, taken for granted.

For the Lord your God has arrived to live among you. He is a mighty Savior. He will give you victory. He will rejoice over you in great gladness; he will love you and not accuse you.

ZEPHANIAH 3:17 TLB

The moms I talk to just want someone to notice, to appreciate what they're doing. To them—and to all of us—these words of Zephaniah speak with quiet assurance. They remind us that there is One who knows all we do—and is right there with us all the time, cheering us on, rejoicing over us with great gladness. He notices your worthy desires and your efforts. He is shouting with joy at all you are doing in his name.

Someone Who *Cares*

Today in Christian circles we hear a lot about the importance of "accountability"—and that's good. We all need someone in our lives who knows us intimately and will hold us responsible for what we do and say. I have a group of friends who do that for me. They love me, they pray for me—but they're also honest with me. When I'm out of line, I can trust them to tell me so.

Being accountable to my group of friends reminds me that I am also accountable to God for my thoughts and actions. He has known me from the very beginning; he knows me through and through. He looks at my public life (my "path") and my private life (my "lying down").

The good news is that both my friends and my heavenly Father hold me accountable because they love me. How can I grow unless somebody knows me and cares what I do?

O Lord, Thou hast searched me and known me.
Thou dost know when I sit down and when I rise up;
Thou dost understand my thought from afar.
Thou dost scrutinize my path and my lying down,
And art intimately acquainted with all my ways.

PSALM 139:1–3 NASB

God Knows
WHAT HE'S DOING!

Just as all created things have a purpose in God's plan, so do the words he has spoken and written in the Scriptures. When God speaks, it's for a purpose, and his words are mighty enough to change the world. (Another passage of scripture says that they are "living and powerful, and sharper than any two-edged sword" (Hebrews 4:12 NASB). We must never doubt that— even when it seems that all of his words are falling on deaf ears and

For as the rain and snow come down
from heaven,
And do not return there without watering
the earth…
So shall My word be which goes forth
from My mouth;
It shall not return to Me empty, without
accomplishing what I desire.

ISAIAH 55:10-11 NASB

that nobody's paying any attention. We can stand fast and know that each letter, each syllable, each word, each sentence, each paragraph will accomplish what God had in mind for it. We can pray confidently for God's will to be done on earth as it is in heaven—because that's exactly what will happen, through God's Word, in his own perfect timing.

GOD *Wants* TO BE FOUND

sometimes have people tell me that they tried to get in touch with me, but couldn't. And I know that's not true—because I'm very accessible. I have dependable voice mail, a website that receives Emails, and a publisher that's good at forwarding letters. I'm conscientious about returning messages. So if people say they couldn't get through to me, I know they haven't been trying very hard.

I think that's true of God, too. He's always available to us if we will seek him. But seeking means more than occasionally attending church or throwing a prayer his way. He wants us to really care about finding him—to put a little heart and soul into our seeking.

But God isn't playing hard to get! He *wants* to be found. And whenever I've come to him in honest need, truly desiring to know him, he's been right there—never late, always caring and comforting. He is there! All I have to do is look.

But, if...you seek the LORD your God, you will find him if you look for him with all your heart and with all your soul.

DEUTERONOMY 4:29 NIV

75

HOPE FOR YOUR *Heart*

I will give you one heart and a new spirit;
I will take from you your hearts of stone
and give you tender hearts of love for God.

EZEKIEL 11:19 TLB

The number one killer in America is death related to heart failure. Americans seem to place tremendous stress upon that fist-sized muscle called the heart. Some is caused by the food we eat, by our high-pressure lifestyles, by lack of physical conditioning. Other health problems can stress our hearts as well. And some hearts—such as those with congenital defects—are less able to handle stress than others.

Spiritually speaking, of course, we all are born with a congenital heart problem. That is, we are all sinners and prone to rebellion from God's plan for our lives. And the more we continue in our own way, the more hardened and scarred our spiritual hearts can become. But we don't have to live that way. God promises that he will give us a new heart and a new spirit—and all this without needles or anesthesia. He can replace our hardened old heart with a tender, loving one. And to take advantage of this wonderful opportunity, all we have to do is surrender our hearts to him. Why wait?

Trouble—
AND BEYOND

Why are so many people surprised when life is difficult? Jesus told us it would be that way! But so many people I meet seem to think they're entitled to a trouble-free life—nothing but happiness, fun, and financial success. Then, when trouble inevitably comes, they're devastated. To me, it seems so much better to expect the problems and let them teach me something…such as what's really important in life.

Through this long bout of discomfort I've had a lot more time to ponder just that. The little things that are free have gone up in my value system—a baby's hug, a sea breeze, a call from a friend. Supposedly big issues such as money and prestige have gone way down. Best of all, I'm learning that it's possible to feel content and peaceful even while bad things are happening—because I know it's all temporary. I can expect pain and trouble because that's part of living in the world, but I can trust God's promise that he'll carry me past it all—that he has overcome this troublesome world.

These things I have spoken to you, that in Me you may have peace. In the world you will have tribulation; but be of good cheer, I have overcome the world.

JOHN 16:33 NKJV

THE BLESSING OF *Believing*

Do you ever have trouble believing in something you haven't seen? The disciple Thomas did. He couldn't bring himself to believe in Jesus' resurrection until he actually saw and touched Jesus. Jesus told Thomas, "Because you have seen me, you have believed; blessed are those who have not seen and yet have believed" (John 20:29 NIV). I don't believe Jesus was scolding Thomas. He was just saying that Thomas would be a lot happier—that's what "blessed" means!—if he could learn to take some things on faith! I think that's

true for me, too. Every day I take it on faith that my car will start, my TV will click on, my Internet website will function. I don't really understand any of these things— they seem like miracles to me! But they work— at least most of the time! So if I can manage to believe in these man-made miracles, why should I have trouble believing in God? Though I haven't physically seen him, I have felt his presence. I have seen his works. I don't want to waste my energy fussing over whether God is real. Instead, I choose to enjoy the blessing of belief.

Now faith is the substance of things hoped for, the evidence of things not seen.

HEBREWS 11:1 NKJV

Plans for the *Future*

For I know the plans I have for you, says the Lord. They are plans for good and not for evil, to give you a future and a hope.

After walking through the valley of the shadow of death for these last two years, I have come to the conclusion that my God has a plan for me, that His plans are for my good, and that they will provide me with a hopeful future. This is true no matter what happens— whether I die tomorrow or live to a ripe old age. I have truly come to believe, as Paul shares in Philippians, that "For me to live is Christ and to die is gain" (Philippians 1:21 NIV). Each additional day that God gives me, I want to know God in a deeper way. And I can't wait to see what his good plans are for me.

No matter what, I know that my cup overflows—that "surely goodness and lovingkindness will follow me all the days of my life, and I will dwell in the house of the Lord forever" (Psalm 23:56 NASB).

A Final *Blessing* for You

*M*y prayer for you would be the same blessing that Moses gave to his brother, Aaron:

May the Lord bless you.
May the Lord keep you always safe
*   in his care.*
May the Lord smile upon you And show
*   you more of himself each day.*
May you feel God's grace—and see
*   his face!*
God's peace to you always!

This is how it works: The more you trust God, the more you'll come to know his character and understand his blessings. More and more, you'll find yourself staring in amazement at what he's done in your life—and waiting in anticipation for what he's going to do next.

The Lord bless you, and keep you;
The Lord make His face shine on you,
And be gracious to you;
The Lord lift up His countenance on you,
And give you peace.

NUMBERS 6:24–26 NASB